Thought Swaps for Secure Attachment

The Thought Swap Series

Thought Swaps for Building Metacognition
Thought Swaps for Setting Boundaries
Thought Swaps for Emotional Availability
Thought Swaps for Adaptability

Thought Swaps for Secure Attachment

*From Anxious or Avoidant
to Secure Thinking*

Lyndsey Getty

This book is part of The Thought Swap Series published in the United States by The Thought Method Co. LLC

www.thoughtswaps.com

DISCLAIMER: The information and advice presented in this book are not meant to replace therapeutic or medical advice.

ISBN 978-1-972391-01-3

Thought: That's just how I think.

Swap: I can replace thoughts that aren't helping me with ones that do.

Contents

The Thoughts Behind Secure Attachment . 11
Values and Assessment 17

Attachment Awareness 25
1. Defining Connection 27
2. Defining Safety 28
3. Defining Trust 29
4. External Validation 31
5. Enoughness 32
6. Growth 33
7. Choosing Partners 35
8. Self-Alignment 36
9. Dependence 37
10. Effort 39
11. Responsibility 40
12. Change 41
13. Getting Triggered 43
14. Give Yourself Compassion 45

Attachment in Action 49
Early Days 51
15. First Impressions 52
16. Feeling a Spark 53
17. Opening Up 55
18. Interpreting Signals 56
19. Interpreting Texts 57
20. Text Cadence 59
21. Double Texts 60

22. Availability.. 61

23. Feeling Ignored 63

24. What Ifs... 64

25. Imagining the Future................................ 65

Getting Closer.. **69**

26. Spending More Time Together 70

27. Thoughts When Apart................................. 71

28. Testing Partners 73

29. Defining the Relationship............................ 74

30. Social Media.. 75

31. Reinforcing Boundaries.............................. 77

32. Playfulness and Fun 78

33. Being Vulnerable...................................... 79

34. Reassurance Seeking................................. 81

35. Communicating Needs................................ 82

36. Support 83

Falling in Love **87**

37. Receiving Love 88

38. Small Gestures 89

39. Needing Space 91

40. Giving Space.. 92

41. Feeling Seen 93

42. Saying I Love You 95

43. Passion and Intimacy 96

44. Feeling Deeply Connected 97

45. Navigating Differences............................... 99

46. Meeting Friends and Family........................ 101

Drifting.. **105**

47. Feeling Taken for Granted 106

48. Addressing Concerns................................. 107

49. First Real Conflict 109

50. Upsetting a Partner 110

51. Taking Ownership 111

52. When You're the Problem 113

53. Repair After Conflict 114

54. Saying Sorry 115

55. Reconnecting After Silence 117

Moving On **121**

56. Growing Apart 122

57. Deciding to Leave 123

58. Ghosting 125

59. Saying Goodbye 126

60. When a Partner Leaves 127

61. Thinking About an Ex 129

62. Heartbreak 131

63. Finding Closure 132

64. Seeing an Ex 133

65. Looking Back 135

66. Starting Over 137

Imperfectly Secure **141**

Triggers and Skills **145**

Templates **161**

Anxious: I need them to like me.

Avoidant: What's the point? People just leave.

Secure: Let's see where this goes.

The Thoughts Behind Secure Attachment

Attachment styles can sound confusing or even intimidating, but they're really just thought habits about how you've been taught to view connection.

So three people could be meeting someone new in the exact same situation, but focusing on very different things.

If you've been taught that your worth depends on what other people think, or that relationships can disappear at any moment, you'll likely have an anxious attachment style. Your focus becomes securing the connection and avoiding rejection. You might think, *I need them to like me.*

If you've been hurt, let down, or taught that people can't be trusted, you likely have an avoidant attachment style. So while you may be interested in someone, your underlying belief is, *What's the point? People just leave.*

And if you've experienced relationships that were generally supportive, dependable, and respectful, you're more likely to have secure attachment.

While you may still wonder if someone likes you or worry about getting hurt, your primary focus is understanding whether the connection is right for you. You'll think, *Let's see where this goes.*

Most attachment books explain attachment but don't show what secure thinking sounds like. You end up with the terminology, but won't know how to think more securely in your own relationships.

Rather than focusing on theory, here you'll see how anxious, avoidant, and secure thoughts interpret the same situations, helping you recognize the thinking patterns behind your reactions and develop a more secure approach to connection.

Note: Relating to both anxious and avoidant tendencies is called disorganized attachment.

Book Setup

Here you'll use a thought-focused approach to learning secure attachment that combines three ideas: thinking is part of skill development, role models help us learn, and comparative thinking makes abstract concepts easier to understand.

This book has three parts:
- **Values and Assessment** to establish your starting point.
- **Awareness** to build self-awareness and see the thinking behind secure connections.
- **In Action** to see what secure attachment looks like in common situations.

Together, these sections help you recognize thought patterns, practice new ways of thinking, and become more secure in your own relationships.

To support your learning, there's material after the conclusion, including common triggers and skills to help you respond more securely. You don't have to focus on everything, but stay curious and explore the content to see what will help you most.

Thought: I'll just read through and see what sticks.

Swap: Taking my time helps me understand and use what I'm learning.

How to Use This Book

The swaps are designed to be straightforward, but changing your thinking rarely is.

1. **Pause.** For each swap, visualize using it in a real situation. Consider:
    - When have I had a similar thought?
    - How would the swap sound in my voice?
    - How would thinking with the swap have changed things?
2. **Reflect.** There are questions throughout the book to help you build awareness and apply what you're learning. You don't have to write your answers, but at least think through each one. Feel free to mark up the pages as you go.
3. **Bridge.** If a swap feels unrealistic, don't force it. So if the thought is, *I need them to like me*, and the swap is, *Let's see where this goes*, a step closer would be, *Do I like them?*
4. **Repeat.** Your current thought patterns have been reinforced over time, so building new ones takes practice. Repeating the swaps or writing them down will help reinforce them.

Values and Assessment

Before building secure attachment, it helps to understand how you currently think about connection. Your values help clarify what matters most to you so you can build secure attachment with greater intention. The self-assessment will help you identify patterns, areas for growth, and opportunities to strengthen your relationships.

Thought: I handled that badly.

Swap: How can I respond in a way that's more aligned with my values next time?

Value Setting

Below are 20 values related to relationships and connection. Circle three that feel most important to you.

Accountability · Respect · Presence
Trust · Honesty · Reliability · Stability
Emotional safety · Consistency · Effort
Patience · Understanding · Acceptance
Support · Affection · Playfulness · Growth
Vulnerability · Openness · Communication

How do you prioritize your values in relationships, and what would help you stay aligned when a situation throws you off track?

____

____

____

____

____

Keep your values in mind as you go through the book.

Thought: This is just how I am.

Swap: When I'm aware of my patterns I can change them.

Self-Assessment

This assessment isn't a diagnosis or a reason to beat yourself up. Rate each statement on a scale of 1 to 5. For the most helpful results, answer honestly and think about how you usually respond rather than how you'd like to respond.

1 = Strongly Disagree   2 = Disagree   3 = Neutral
4 = Agree   5 = Strongly Agree

In a relationship, you...   **Score**

1. Focus more on whether someone likes you than if you like them   ______

2. Think about a partner's flaws when the relationship starts feeling too close   ______

3. Change how you act to keep someone interested   ______

4. Focus on how something was said instead of what was said   ______

5. Feel relieved when plans get canceled or you unexpectedly get space   ______

6. Avoid expressing your needs or setting boundaries because you worry it might push someone away   ______

7. Think about the relationship repeatedly when something feels uncertain   ______

In a relationship, you...   **Score**

8. Re-read texts or conversations to figure out what someone meant _______

9. Believe people should handle their own emotions _______

10. Think a partner is being "too emotional" when they want to talk about feelings _______

11. Assume something's wrong if communication slows or changes _______

12. Watch a partner's tone or behavior for signs they may be pulling away _______

13. Keep personal struggles to yourself _______

14. Change the subject or joke when conversations become emotionally serious _______

15. Feel responsible for keeping the relationship stable _______

16. Pull away when a relationship requires more emotional openness _______

Scoring

Add up your scores for each group.

X: 1 + 3 + 6 + 7 + 8 + 11 + 12 + 15 = _______
V: 2 + 4 + 5 + 9 + 10 + 13 + 14 + 16 = _______

Each score ranges from 8 to 40.
- **16 or less X & V** secure tendencies
- **More than 16 X:** anxious tendencies
- **More than 16 V:** avoidant tendencies
- **More than 16 in both:** disorganized tendencies

What patterns did you notice while filling out the assessment? How do these patterns influence your behaviors in connections? How does it feel knowing you can build a more secure attachment style?

____

____

____

____

____

____

How would you ideally approach relationships? What is your goal for building secure attachment?

____

____

____

____

Attachment Awareness

Attachment awareness includes understanding how you think about connection, how you respond to closeness and distance, and recognizing the habits that influence your relationships. As you go through this section, pay attention to the patterns you recognize in yourself and consider where you learned them.

Each style is looking for connection, safety, and trust. The difference is how you've learned to define those concepts. If you grew up feeling accepted and supported, you learned that relationships are generally safe and dependable. If connection was inconsistent, unpredictable, or unavailable, you learned to worry about being rejected, keep people at a distance, or move back and forth between the two. Over time, these beliefs become automatic thoughts that influence how you interpret situations, respond to uncertainty, and approach relationships.

Anxious: If the connection isn't intense, the relationship isn't real.

Avoidant: If I don't have space, I'm not safe.

Secure: It won't always feel exciting.

Anxious: If they just reassured me more, I'd finally feel secure.

Avoidant: If they backed off, I'd feel more in control.

Secure: I don't know how this will go, but I'll be okay either way.

Anxious: People can be unpredictable. I have to pay attention so I don't get hurt.

Avoidant: I can trust people as long as I'm the one setting the terms.

Secure: There are people I can trust.

Attachment styles are influenced by the messages you hear about relationships in your environment, including music, movies, television, social media, and the people around you. You may hear that you need someone to complete you, that you're not enough, or that you need to become perfect before you're worthy of love. It's much less common to hear secure messages that remind you that you're already enough and that relationships can add to your life without defining your worth.

Anxious: I'm nobody until somebody loves me.

Avoidant: Needing someone makes me weak.

Secure: I love being liked, but it doesn't decide my worth.

Anxious: I'm too much to be loved the way I want.

Avoidant: I'm not able to give someone what they need.

Secure: I have a lot to give.

Growth

Anxious: No one will want me until I'm perfect.

Avoidant: I can't get close until I've figured myself out.

Secure: I can grow while still letting people know me.

There's an idea that you're drawn to certain people because you're trying to fix or redo your childhood. It's more likely that you're used to certain patterns, don't realize there are other options, and stay in what feels familiar.

Anxious: Why do I always want the person who leaves me guessing where I stand?

Avoidant: I like people who fit into my life without adding pressure or obligation.

Secure: I'm choosing someone who reflects what I value.

Anxious: I'll become who they want me to be. I just want it to work.

Avoidant: I'll keep people out so I don't lose myself.

Secure: I'll stay connected without abandoning myself.

Anxious: I'm too needy. I probably ruin everything.

Avoidant: Depending on someone usually leads to disappointment.

Secure: I love independence and connection.

Secure attachment isn't just about how you view relationships. It's about choosing thoughts that support connection, growth, and change.

Anxious: If it's hard, I must be the problem.

Avoidant: If there's conflict, it's not worth it.

Secure: Stuff happens. How we manage it is what matters.

Responsibility

Anxious: This is why I'm like this. I've had bad experiences.

Avoidant: That's just how I was raised. It is what it is.

Secure: I choose how I respond now.

Anxious: I can't stop focusing on what I'm doing wrong. Knowing this just confirms something's wrong with me.

Avoidant: This just proves I'm not built for relationships.

Secure: Glad I can change these patterns.

Changing your thoughts is gradual, so you may still get triggered and respond from old patterns. Noticing you're triggered is progress and part of building awareness. Over time, the gap between awareness and action gets shorter, and secure thinking becomes more automatic.

Anxious: If I still get triggered, does that mean I haven't healed?

Avoidant: I hate that this still affects me. I don't want to feel this.

Secure: I'm noticing. That's progress.

Learning that you have anxious or avoidant tendencies can feel like a shock. You might feel the urge to blame yourself, but it's important to have self-compassion.

Anxious: Why am I still like this? I should be further along by now.

Avoidant: I keep pulling away. This is just who I am.

Secure: _______________________

____

____

____

Secure attachment develops through practice. Each time you challenge an insecure thought, communicate openly, or stay engaged instead of falling into old patterns, you're reinforcing a new way of relating to yourself and others. Over time, you'll become more comfortable tolerating uncertainty, communicating directly, and evaluating relationships based on what is actually happening rather than what you fear might happen.

Pause & Reflect

What thoughts are keeping you from secure connection? When do those beliefs impact you most, and how do they influence your behaviors? What can you focus on to build more secure connections?

Attachment in Action

Here you'll move through common relationship situations and see thoughts that shape each stage. Pay attention to familiar patterns and how they influence what you feel and how you act. Notice how a more secure way of thinking would change the way you respond and interact with others. The situations won't always match your experiences exactly. Focus on the thinking behind each example and consider how it applies to your own relationships.

Early Days

Meeting someone with potential is exciting. It can also be unnerving. At this point you know you're interested, but there's still a lot of unknowns, leaving a lot of room for interpretation.

Anxious: How do I get them to like me?

Avoidant: Better to keep a little distance so they don't expect too much.

Secure: They seem interesting!

Anxious: Did I say too much? Are they judging me? Do they feel it too? Am I reading this wrong?

Avoidant: This is fun, but I'm not getting too invested.

Secure: This is exciting. I'm probably grinning like an idiot.

Opening up can feel risky when your thoughts focus more on avoiding rejection than building connection.

Anxious: What if I say too much and scare them away?

Avoidant: I'll share a little, but not too much.

Secure: I'm nervous, but I want them to truly know me.

Anxious: Did that mean something, or am I overthinking it?

Avoidant: It's probably nothing.

Secure: I think they're interested. I'll be clear that I am too.

Anxious: That last text felt cold. I must have done something wrong.

Avoidant: I can't tell what they mean, so I'm just going to ignore it.

Secure: That felt off. I can ask or leave it.

The way you think about communication influences what response times mean to you. The same situation can feel reassuring, stressful, or overwhelming depending on the thoughts you attach to it.

Anxious: If we're not talking all the time, something's wrong.

Avoidant: Too much texting makes me feel trapped.

Secure: We'll figure out a rhythm that works.

Anxious: I'll text again, maybe they just didn't see it, or will that look too needy?

Avoidant: If I seem too interested, I'll lose my sense of control.

Secure: If I have something to say, I'll text.

Anxious: If they care, they should always be available.

Avoidant: I want them available when it works for me.

Secure: We don't need constant contact to stay connected.

Thinking "they're ignoring me" is a conclusion drawn from a gap. Noticing you've jumped to that conclusion is the first step to choosing a different interpretation.

Anxious: They're ignoring me on purpose.

Avoidant: It's easier when people keep their distance.

Secure: They might be busy.

Anxious: What if they lose interest? What if I said the wrong thing? What if this never goes anywhere?

Avoidant: Whatever happens, happens.

Secure: I don't know how this will go yet.

Anxious: This could be everything. I can already imagine a future with them.

Avoidant: Thinking ahead feels like too much.

Secure: I'm excited to see where this goes.

In the early stages of connection, there's a lot to think about. It's easy to get sidetracked by wanting to be chosen or assigning meaning to gaps in information. You might find yourself preparing for rejection or protecting yourself from getting too close. Secure attachment is staying open to connection while still prioritizing your values and considering whether someone is a good fit for your relationship goals.

Pause & Reflect

What thoughts do you tend to default to when you first like someone? How do those thoughts get you off track? How can you prioritize more secure thinking at the beginning of connection?

____

____

____

____

____

____

Getting Closer

As you start to get closer, it's less about whether you like each other and more about if you're truly compatible. The shared destination is still secure connection, but it's approached differently based on how you think about needs.

Anxious: Am I staying too long? Am I bothering them?

Avoidant: This is too much time together. I should probably head out.

Secure: I like this, and I'll make time for myself later.

Anxious: Are they thinking about me? Do they miss me?

Avoidant: I can't say I miss them; it would give them too much power.

Secure: I miss them.

Testing usually starts with a thought like "I can't ask directly, so I'll find out another way." It can feel protective, but it's not, and it keeps you from learning direct communication.

Anxious: If they really care, they'll pass this test I've set up in my head.

Avoidant: I'll pull away and see if they seem needy or pressure me.

Secure: I don't need to test this.

Anxious: What are we? I need to know where this is going, but I don't want to scare them off.

Avoidant: Why do we need to label it?

Secure: I want to talk about where this is going.

Anxious: They posted their friends but not me. Does that mean something?

Avoidant: I don't want people reading into our relationship online.

Secure: I'll ask how they want to handle posting.

It's hard to hold a boundary you don't think you deserve.

Anxious: If I say no, they might get upset.

Avoidant: It's easier not to deal with this right now.

Secure: I can say what I need.

Anxious: I hope they think I'm fun.

Avoidant: This is nice, but I don't want them to always expect it to be like this.

Secure: I like how easy this feels.

Anxious: What if I share this and they don't respond well?

Avoidant: It's easier to keep things light.

Secure: I want them to know this about me.

The actual act of asking for reassurance is easy. What makes it difficult are the thoughts you have around reassurance, like thinking it makes you weak or that needing reassurance says something negative about you.

Anxious: If I don't ask, I'll spiral. If I do ask, I'll seem too needy.

Avoidant: If I need reassurance, it means something must be wrong with me.

Secure: I can ask for reassurance.

Anxious: Maybe I'm asking for too much.

Avoidant: It's probably not worth bringing this up.

Secure: This matters to me, I'll say something.

Anxious: What if I'm too much for them or my problems push them away?

Avoidant: I don't want to burden them. I'll deal with this myself.

Secure: I'm going through something hard, I'm glad they're here.

As relationships become more established, needs become harder to avoid. Thinking your needs are too much can prevent honest conversations about compatibility and keep you in relationships that aren't a good fit. Secure attachment involves expressing your needs and giving others the opportunity to meet them.

Pause & Reflect

Have you ever felt uncomfortable asserting a boundary or letting someone know what you need or want? Where do you hold back instead of being direct? What would a clear, secure version of you say in that moment?

____

____

____

____

____

____

____

Falling in Love

Falling in love is exciting but it can also make the stakes feel higher. Thoughts during this stage shift from whether your needs are being met to the possibility of being left— even if you don't realize it on the surface.

Anxious: They couldn't really love me if they knew everything.

Avoidant: If I let this in, they might see who I really am and not like it.

Secure: They can care about me, I don't need to question it.

Anxious: Did they notice? Was it enough?

Avoidant: I'll do something nice, but it doesn't need to be a big thing.

Secure: I like doing things for them.

The anxious thought when a partner needs space is almost always "this is about me." The avoidant thought triggering the need for space is often "if I don't pull back, I'll lose myself in this."

Anxious: I can't take space, they'll think I'm mad at them or pulling away.

Avoidant: When I need space, I'll vanish. It's just easier.

Secure: I'll let them know I need some space. It doesn't mean anything's wrong.

Anxious: If they need space, it must mean I did something wrong.

Avoidant: I don't need to know what they're going through. I'm fine alone.

Secure: They just need space, it's not about me.

Anxious: Now they know I'm not perfect. What if they start looking for someone else?

Avoidant: I'll just pretend it was nothing. No need to make it a big deal.

Secure: It feels nice to feel seen.

*Saying I love you
for the first time is
vulnerable for everyone.
Your attachment style
shapes whether that
vulnerability feels
exciting, terrifying, or
unnecessary.*

Anxious: I think I should tell them, but what if they don't say it back?

Avoidant: I feel it, but there's no need to say it.

Secure: I'm excited to tell them.

Anxious: Was that good for them? Do I need to do more?

Avoidant: That was great, but I'm not reading too much into it.

Secure: I love how close we feel.

Anxious: This feels too good to be true. What if I lose this?

Avoidant: We're close, but I need to make sure I don't lose myself.

Secure: I feel really comfortable with them.

Differences become harder to navigate when you think they mean something's wrong.

Anxious: What if our differences become a problem? Should I change?

Avoidant: Maybe we're just too different.

Secure: We don't have to agree on everything.

Introducing other people to the relationship can make anyone feel nervous. Different interpretations lead to different priorities. Anxious is worried about being liked. Avoidant doesn't want to seem too invested. Secure manages the nervousness with a more balanced perspective.

Anxious: What if I say something embarrassing or they don't like me?

Avoidant: This feels like a big step. I don't want them to get the wrong idea.

Secure: I'm nervous, but excited.

It's hard to get truly close when part of you is already preparing for the relationship to end. Falling in love securely means letting someone in without knowing how or if it will end.

Pause & Reflect

When things feel good, do your thoughts stay in the moment or do you focus on what could go wrong? Did you notice any areas where you tend to hold yourself back? What would it be like to think securely and stay open instead of protecting yourself?

Drifting

Most relationships go through a period where things feel less certain than they used to. Connection starts to feel different, and you might question if things are ending. How much weight you put on these shifts influences whether you face them directly or avoid them.

Anxious: Do they even notice everything I do?

Avoidant: I'm done putting in effort.

Secure: I want to talk and see their perspective.

Anxious: They'll think I'm too sensitive if I say this bothered me.

Avoidant: If I name this, I become the problem.

Secure: I can say this bothered me without making it a big deal.

How you interpret conflict determines whether it feels like part of the relationship or a threat to it.

Anxious: It's over. I knew this was too good to be true.

Avoidant: This is why I don't get too close.

Secure: Disagreements happen. We can work through this.

Anxious: If they're upset, it must be my fault.

Avoidant: Whatever. I can't do anything right. I'm done trying.

Secure: I can look at my part without taking all the blame or shutting down.

Anxious: I didn't mean to hurt them. What if I'm the problem?

Avoidant: They're overreacting. I didn't ask for this.

Secure: I'll focus on staying open even if I feel defensive.

Sometimes feedback is a bid for connection. Taking responsibility starts with seeing feedback as information, not a verdict on who you are.

Anxious: I messed everything up. They're going to think I'm terrible.

Avoidant: Bringing this up will only make it worse. I'll pretend it's not a big deal.

Secure: I made a mistake. I'll take responsibility and do better.

Anxious: If we reconnect too soon, maybe we're skipping over what happened.

Avoidant: Once conflict happens, I detach. I don't want to revisit it.

Secure: Repair takes time, it doesn't need to be rushed.

Anxious: I'll just say sorry to keep the peace, I'm sure I did something wrong somehow.

Avoidant: I don't apologize. I didn't do anything wrong, or they made me do it.

Secure: I'll take responsibility, but I won't take on what isn't mine.

"I'm still here. I just need a little time to process. I'll reach out when I'm ready."

Anxious: Should I reach out first?

Avoidant: I'm not saying anything. They'll reach out when they're ready to move on.

Secure: I'll reach out when I'm ready to talk.

Conflict and distance get interpreted differently by whoever experiences them. Anxious thinking assigns blame to themselves, avoidant thinking assigns it away from themselves, and secure thinking owns what's theirs without taking on all of the responsibility. Repair depends less on what happened and more on whether both people can stay in the conversation long enough to sort it out.

Pause & Reflect

What thoughts do you tend to have when there's distance in a relationship? Do you take on too much, avoid it, or respond clearly? What thoughts would help you respond without over-apologizing or pulling away?

____

____

____

____

____

____

____

Moving On

Breakups are hard. How you think about them can make them even harder.

Anxious: We're drifting. How do I stop this? Should I try harder?

Avoidant: We're not the same anymore. Maybe I shouldn't be in relationships.

Secure: It's unfortunate, but we're not going in the same direction.

Anxious: Walking away means I failed or gave up too soon.

Avoidant: I stayed too long before. I won't do it again.

Secure: Love sometimes means staying. Other times it's letting go.

Ghosting starts with the thought that disappearing is kinder than explaining.
It isn't.

Anxious: I want to say something, but I don't want to seem dramatic.

Avoidant: Ghosting is easier. I don't want the emotional mess.

Secure: I'd rather be clear than just disappear.

Anxious: What if this is a mistake? What if I regret this forever?

Avoidant: It's over. Time to never look back.

Secure: It's the right choice.

Anxious: This just proves there's something wrong with me.

Avoidant: This is why connection isn't worth it.

Secure: This hurts, but I'll get through it.

The story you tell about your ex says more about your thought pattern than it does about them.

Anxious: They were perfect, I can't stop thinking about them. Actually, I hate them.

Avoidant: I don't think about them at all.

Secure: We were together for a reason.

Secure attachment is sometimes misread as not caring. That's actually an avoidant response.

Anxious: I'll never find love again. That was my only chance.

Avoidant: I'm fine. I'll just shove this feeling in a box and pretend it's not there.

Secure: I need time to process.

Anxious: I need answers before I can move on.

Avoidant: I don't need closure; I'll just ignore my feelings.

Secure: I can make peace with how it ended.

Anxious: Do they miss me? Should I say something? What if they moved on and I haven't?

Avoidant: I'll just act like I don't care.

Secure: I can be kind without reopening the past.

Breakups are easier when you don't turn them into self-judgment. You know you did your best and that it just didn't work out.

Anxious: I did so much for them, even things I didn't want to do. And it still wasn't enough.

Avoidant: I kept so much of myself back that I never really gave it a chance.

Secure: I'm glad we tried.

Starting over begins with the thought that what you learned is worth more than what you lost.

Anxious: What if I make the same mistakes again?

Avoidant: I'm better off alone.

Secure: I learned more about what I want. I'll try again when I'm ready.

*Endings are usually centered on
the other person. Anxious
thinking focuses on getting a
partner back or understanding
why they left. Avoidant thinking
concentrates on a partner's
flaws while minimizing their
own contribution to the
relationship. Secure thinking
asks what can be learned from
the experience. To build secure
connection, it's important to
look at your own patterns and
decide what you want to do
differently next time.*

Pause & Reflect

What did you like and not like about your past relationships? What did they show you about your needs? What would it look like to choose a partner based on what you want instead of what feels automatic?

____

____

____

____

____

____

Imperfectly Secure

Most of us were never taught how to change our thought habits so growth can feel unfamiliar at first. Ideally, the process wouldn't be so uncomfortable, but the more thought work you do, the easier it gets.

There will likely be moments where you didn't respond the way you wanted. You might forget the secure thought in the moment only to recognize it later. And you might think, *This isn't for me, I can't be secure*. Ironically, doubt typically means you're close to change.

During the process you might remember some embarrassing things you did when your thought patterns were leading you to anxious or avoidant tendencies. I've sent so many anxious texts, it used to make me cringe. The cringe is part of growth and a sign you would choose differently now.

Change also isn't a straight line. One day you might be feeling secure, and the next thing you know, something triggers an old pattern.

You may also notice that you fall back into old habits in certain situations. This can feel upsetting, but it's actually an opportunity to identify the thoughts holding you back so you can change them. Try to use that information instead of feeling defeated. Pay attention to what's triggering it and consider why.

Remember, the goal isn't to be perfectly secure. It's to move in that direction more often than not. Even secure people have anxious or avoidant tendencies. The difference is how they respond. When a secure person makes a mistake, instead of thinking they can never recover, they have self-compassion and focus on doing better next time.

You've built awareness here, but it won't fully process difficult or traumatic events that lead to your attachment style. Some experiences can carry strong emotional weight. If you find yourself having intense emotional responses or struggling to build secure connections, working with a therapist can help you get the support you need (it helped me a lot).

As you reflect, you might think about past relationships or people you feel the urge to reconnect with. Before reaching out, consider whether reopening that connection aligns with what you're working toward.

You're not responsible for showing someone a different attachment pattern, and the most meaningful thing you can do is continue to improve your own.

We focused on relationships with others, but the most important one you're repairing is the relationship you have with yourself.

This is a book you can come back to, and the swaps are meant to be revisited. Keep it nearby and use it when you need it. I do.

Every time you notice a pattern and choose differently, you move closer to secure connection.

Triggers and Skills

If you want more than awareness, this section breaks down the triggers behind common reactions in relationships. It also gives you practical ways to build the core skills behind secure attachment so you can manage your responses.

Triggers

A trigger is a stimulus that creates an emotional response. It can be positive, like smelling cookies and feeling excited; neutral, like noticing the smell without any emotional shift; or negative, like smelling cookies and realizing you can't have them because you're allergic.

Triggers are tied to past experiences. In relationships, common triggers include closeness, rejection, and uncertainty. So if you had caregivers who were emotionally unavailable and shut down bids for closeness, connection in relationships may trigger discomfort or unease. But if your caregivers were open and responsive, closeness is more likely to feel safe and positive.

It's important to understand these triggers because once you recognize them, you can change how you respond. If you don't, you'll likely repeat the same relationship patterns with different people.

Learning to recognize triggers is the first step. Here are examples to get started, then use the skills section to learn how to manage them.

Closeness is triggered when you feel a connection or attachment to someone. For some, closeness is comforting. For others, it creates unease, especially if past closeness led to hurt. It can also bring up concern or worry about losing a connection that feels important.

Common signs of a closeness trigger:
- noticing you're prioritizing time with or around the person
- adjusting your schedule or routines to include them
- feeling a change in your baseline mood after interactions

How it can show up in behavior:
- reaching out more, asking for reassurance, or trying to deepen the connection
- delaying responses, craving more alone time, or creating space after interactions
- continuing to engage consistently without changing your pace or behavior

Rejection is triggered when a connection feels at risk or when you feel judged. Even if you tell yourself you don't care, connection is a basic need, so rejection can feel threatening. Repeated experiences of rejection can make this response stronger, but it can affect anyone.

Common signs of a rejection trigger:
- perceiving less effort, attention, or engagement from the other person
- becoming more aware of how you're being perceived or evaluated
- feeling a change in how secure or stable the connection feels

How it can show up in behavior:
- increasing effort, questioning, analyzing, or trying to confirm what changed
- stepping back, lowering effort, redirecting focus to other people, tasks, or priorities
- maintaining the same behavior while watching for consistency over time

Uncertainty is triggered when connection is unclear and you don't know where you stand. It can feel uncomfortable because most people haven't learned how to regulate without answers. Past experiences of not knowing where you stood can make uncertainty feel more intense.

Common signs of an uncertainty trigger:
- becoming more aware of gaps, mixed signals, or unanswered questions
- feeling a shift in how stable or predictable the interaction seems
- recognizing you're trying to figure out what something means

How it can show up in behavior:
- filling in the gaps with assumptions or possible outcomes
- distracting yourself or shifting focus away from the situation
- continuing to engage while allowing the situation to remain unclear, or asking questions for clarity

Managing Triggers

Managing a trigger starts with naming it. When you can say "this is uncertainty" or "this is fear of rejection," you depersonalize and create space between you and the reaction.

From there, pause before responding. Give yourself a moment to settle, even if that's just slowing down, taking a breath, or giving yourself a small form of comfort, like a hug.

Then look at what's actually happening in the present instead of being tangled in past experiences. You can also choose not to decide right away and give the situation space before responding.

Skills

The skills in this book are areas you can strengthen to respond more securely. Each one targets a different part of how you think, feel, and act in relationships.

Building any skill isn't clean or predictable, but the more you practice, the easier it becomes. Staying focused on your values and what you can control gives you room to keep improving without expecting it to feel perfect.

As you read about the skills, you'll notice they overlap and build on each other. Emotional awareness helps with emotional regulation, emotional regulation helps with uncertainty tolerance and direct communication.

The process is messy. As you continue to work on changing your thought patterns and responses, you build self-awareness, which helps you build the skills.

Emotional awareness is recognizing what you feel while staying separate from it. When you can name what you feel clearly, you're less likely to be pulled into it. That awareness becomes the starting point for a more intentional response.

You can build awareness by:
1. Reverse engineering when you felt emotionally charged. Think back to a time you had a strong emotional reaction and ask what you were feeling at the time.
2. Separating yourself from emotion and seeing it as a signal. Instead of saying "I'm anxious," you shift to "I'm noticing feelings of anxiety." That wording creates space between you and the emotion.

Looking up emotions and what they feel like can help. I personally love Brené Brown's *Atlas of the Heart*. It is like an encyclopedia for emotions.

Emotional regulation is staying steady enough to choose how you respond. Awareness feeds directly into this. When you name an emotion, you create enough distance to pause and consider it instead of reacting. From there, you can ask why the emotion is present and what it's pointing to.

You can work on emotional regulation by:
1. Reverse engineering when you've reacted strongly due to an emotional charge and how responding more in line with your goals and values might have changed the outcome
2. Reflect on when you've had strong emotional responses and ask what previous experience triggered it. The more you reflect, the better you'll get at stopping in the moment to ask where the emotion is coming from.
3. Pause before responding. Give yourself time before reacting, even if that means stepping away, taking a breath, or waiting to reply.

Uncertainty tolerance is staying steady when you don't have clear answers. Most people aren't taught how to handle uncertainty, so it feels like something to avoid rather than something to work with. But life and relationships are unpredictable, so uncertainty is something you need to learn to manage.

You can build uncertainty tolerance by:
1. Reminding yourself that life is unpredictable and allowing time or situations to develop.
2. Focusing on what you can control, like asking for more information or using emotional regulation techniques to manage your feelings of discomfort around uncertainty.
3. Sitting in the discomfort by actively acknowledging it's there and that it's not ideal, but it is part of connection and relationships.
4. Giving yourself the gentle reminder that the more you work to manage uncertainty, the easier it becomes to sit with it.

Direct communication is expressing what you think, feel, and need. It sounds simple, and you may feel confident when you play out a conversation in the shower, but communicating your needs in person can feel intimidating or scary.

You can work on direct communication by:
1. Truly considering your needs and what you want and don't want in your relationships.
2. Identifying what needs have gone unmet in past relationships.
3. Practicing what you want to say in the mirror or expressing your needs to a therapist or AI platform and asking for help stating them clearly and assertively without being rigid.

Trust is allowing connection without trying to control the outcome. It includes trusting yourself to handle what happens and trusting others based on what they consistently do, not what you hope they'll do.

1. Think back to times when you worked through a difficult situation and remind yourself that you can trust yourself to handle challenges again.
2. Consider the trustworthy people in your life. If none come to mind, think of a time when you trusted someone and it worked out.
3. Remind yourself that it's important to allow trust to build and strengthen as connections deepen.
4. Ask yourself how you try to control situations or people and what it would look like to stop.

Continual Growth

Like learning an instrument or a sport, interpersonal skills build with repetition and practice.

The most important thing is meeting yourself where you're at and having self-compassion during the process. Some people may already be aware of their emotions and can move right into managing them, while others may need to first accept that emotions aren't weakness before feeling comfortable addressing or admitting they have them.

If you're like me, you may need to work on identifying your needs before directly communicating them.

No matter where you're at in the process, building these skills will help in every area of life, and when you focus on improving them, you also improve the most important relationship there is: the one you have with yourself.

Templates

Situation: _______________________

Thought: _______________________

____

____

____

Swap: _______________________

____

____

____

Situation: _______________________

Thought: _______________________

____

____

____

Swap: _______________________

____

____

____

Notes

Share Your Swaps

Seeing how others approach the same situations can help more people learn to think securely. Post your favorite thought swap, or one of your own, on TikTok and tag @thoughtswaps. I'd love to see what you come up with.

Leave a Review

Reviews help others find The Thought Swaps Series and support independent authors like me. If you enjoyed this book, please leave a review on Amazon, Goodreads, or StoryGraph.

Want more thought swaps? Visit thoughtswaps.com for the full series.

The Thoughtbook Series

Available on Amazon

The Thought Swaps Series

Available on Amazon

About the Author

Photo by YEE

Lyndsey Getty is the creator of thought literacy. She's on a mission to help people build healthier relationships with their thoughts. Her work is driven by the belief that many challenges can be improved by changing how we think about ourselves, others, and our experiences. She values practical application over theory and believes skills are built through awareness, effort, and practice. Recurring themes throughout her work include self-awareness, personal growth, stronger relationships, and the idea that small shifts in thinking can create meaningful change over time.

www.thoughtswaps.com
thoughtswaps@gmail.com
@thoughtswaps on TikTok

You Shouldn't Need a PhD to Understand Your Thoughts

Thought literacy is the skill of deliberate thinking. This book uses Thought Swaps, a thought-literate approach, to help you build secure attachment.

Learn more at www.thoughtliteracy.org

9 781972 391013